NATIONAL TESTS practice papers

FOR THE YEAR 2005

Maths, English and Science

Book 1 Levels 3–5

practice papers

AGE 10–11
Key Stage 2

Contents	Page
Introduction	
The National Tests: A Summary	iii
Maths Test	
Maths at Key Stage 2	1
Test A (without calculator)	2
Test B (with calculator)	11
Mental Maths Test Questions	20
Mental Maths Test Answer Sheet	21
Answers	22
National Curriculum Levels	26
English Test	
Reading Test	27
Writing Test	43
Spelling Test	47
Answers	49
National Curriculum Levels	51
Science Test	
Science at Key Stage 2	52
Science Test	53
Answers	61
National Curriculum Levels	62

Acknowledgements
The Publishers would like to thank the following for permission to reproduce copyright material:

"Christmas Eve", from *Her Benny*, Silas Hocking, Memories Paperback, 1994

"A Week to Christmas" by John Cotton

Every effort has been made to trace all copyright holders, but if any have been inadvertently overlooked, the Publishers will be pleased to make the necessary arrangements at the first opportunity.

First published in 2005
exclusively for WHSmith by
Hodder Murray,
a member of the Hodder Headline Group
338 Euston Road
London NW1 3BH

Text © Hodder Murray 2005

All rights reserved. Apart from any use permitted under UK copyright law, no part of this publication may be reproduced or transmitted in any form or by any means, electronic or mechanical, including photocopying, recording, or any information storage and retrieval system, without permission in writing from the publisher or under licence from the Copyright Licensing Agency Limited. Further details of such licences (for reprographic reproduction) may be obtained from the Copyright Licensing Agency Limited, of 90 Tottenham Court Road, London W1T 4LP.

Authors: Steve Mills and Hilary Koll (Maths); Christine Moorcroft and Ray Barker (English); Graham Peacock (Science)

Impression   5 4 3 2 1
Year   2006 2005

Printed and bound in Spain

A catalogue record for this title is available from the British Library

ISBN 0 340 88850 4

NOTE: The tests, questions and advice in this book are not reproductions of the official test materials sent to schools. The official testing process is supported by guidance and training for teachers in setting and marking tests and interpreting the results. The results achieved in the tests in this book may not be the same as those achieved in the official tests.

Introduction

The National Tests: A Summary

What are the National Tests?

Children who attend state schools in England sit National Tests (also known as SATs) at the ages of 7, 11 and 14. Those at ages 11 and 14 are taken at the beginning of May. Those at age 7 can be carried out at any point during the year, as chosen by the teacher. Children in Wales may take the same tests at 11 and 14. All children may also sit optional tests in the intervening years – many schools have chosen to adopt these tests.

The results are used by the school to assess each child's level of knowledge and progress in English and Maths at Key Stage 1 and English, Maths and Science at Key Stages 2 and 3. They also provide useful guidance for the child's next teacher.

The educational calendar for children aged 5–14 is structured as follows:

Key Stage	Year	Age by end of year	National Test
1 (KS1)	1	6	
	2	7	KEY STAGE 1
2 (KS2)	3	8	Optional Year 3
	4	9	Optional Year 4
	5	10	Optional Year 5
	6	11	KEY STAGE 2
3 (KS3)	7	12	
	8	13	
	9	14	KEY STAGE 3

Levels

National average levels have been set for children's results in the National Tests. The levels are as follows:

LEVEL	AGE 7 (Key Stage 1)	AGE 11 (Key Stage 2)	AGE 14 (Key Stage 3)
8			
7			
6			
5			
4			
3			
2			
2a			
2b			
2c			
1			

- BELOW EXPECTED LEVEL
- EXPECTED LEVEL
- ABOVE EXPECTED LEVEL
- EXCEPTIONAL

Introduction

Test Timetable

Key Stage 2 tests take place in one week in May. All children sit the same test at the same time. In 2005, the tests will take place in the week of **9–13 May**. Your child's school will be able to provide you with a detailed timetable.

Results

Your child's school will send you a report indicating his or her levels in the tests and the teacher assessment.

The school's overall test results will be included in local and national league tables, which are published in most newspapers.

What can parents do to help?

While it is never a good idea to encourage cramming, you can help your child to succeed by:

- Making sure he or she has enough food, sleep and leisure time during the test period.
- Encouraging him or her to practise important skills such as writing and reading stories, spelling and mental maths.
- Telling him or her what to expect in the test, such as important symbols and key words.
- Helping him or her to be comfortable in test conditions including working within a time limit, reading questions carefully and understanding different ways of answering.

Maths Test

Maths at Key Stage 2

The Key Stage 2 National Tests cover Number, Measures, Shape and Space, and Data Handling. Most children will take two one-hour written tests and a short, orally delivered mental test. Test A is a written non-calculator paper and Test B is a written paper where children can use a calculator, should they wish.

Levels

Children taking the Maths Tests A and B and the Mental Maths Test can achieve below Level 3, Level 3, Level 4 or Level 5, with a typical 11-year-old attaining Level 4.

To gain an idea of the level at which your child is working, use the table on page 26, which shows you how to convert your child's marks into a National Curriculum Level.

Setting the tests

Written tests

Allow one hour for each test. Do not expect your child to take them one after another. In the National Test week, children will take the mathematics tests over two or three days.

Your child will need a ruler, pencil, eraser, protractor and, if possible, a small mirror or piece of tracing paper, together with a calculator (for Test B).

Encourage your child to work systematically through each test, returning later to questions which cause difficulty.

If your child has difficulty in reading the questions, you can read them aloud, provided the mathematical words are not altered or explained. Where necessary, your child can dictate answers and these can be written down for him or her. For large numbers, however, your child should be clear which digits are intended to be written, e.g. for a number such as three thousand and six, your child should indicate that this is written as three, zero, zero, six.

Mental Maths Test

The mental test should take approximately 10–15 minutes to give, by reading aloud the questions on page 20, which you should copy for your own use while your child writes on page 21. Your child will only need a pencil and an eraser for the mental test.

Allow only the time suggested for each question. You may read each one twice within this time.

Marking the tests

Next to each question in the written tests is a number indicating how many marks the question or part of the question is worth. Enter your child's mark into the circle above this, using the answer pages (22–25) to help you decide how many points to award.

Find your child's total score from the written tests and mental test, then refer to page 26 for information about the level your child might be working at.

Maths Test
Test A (without calculator)

1 Fill in the missing numbers.

a 18 ÷ ☐6☐ = 3

b 12 + 15 = 38 − ☐11☐

c (2 × 20) − ☐4☐ = 10 + ☐30☐

2 Write two more numbers into this diagram so that the numbers in each row and column add up to 100.

10 60 30
50 40 10
40 20 40

3 a Continue this sequence.

1 3 6 10 ☐ ☐

b Explain how you worked out the missing numbers.

_____

_____

_____

Maths Test A

4 At a netball tournament there are 7 players in each team.

112 players take part in the tournament.

How many teams take part in the tournament?

2

5 Lucy is playing darts. She throws three darts and hits **three different** numbers. She notices that the **mean** of the numbers is **9**.

What **different** numbers could Lucy have hit?

1

TOTAL

3

Maths Test A

6 A shop sells ice cream.

This table shows the most popular types of ice cream sold in the shop during one day.

Flavour	Large cone	Small cone
Chocolate	15	14
Vanilla	19	12
Strawberry	11	8

a How many **small** cones were sold during the day?

b Which flavour had 31 cones sold during the day?

7 One side of a shape has been drawn below. The shape has **three right angles** and **more than four sides**. Using a ruler, draw the other sides to complete the shape.

Maths Test A

8 Mr Thomas bought three shirts.

a One shirt cost £4.25. The second shirt cost twice as much.

How much did the second shirt cost?

£ ☐

b Mr Thomas spent exactly £20 on all three shirts.

How much did the third shirt cost?

£ ☐

9 Fill in the missing numbers so the numbers along all three sides have the same total.

```
         4.5
        /   \
       ☐     ☐
      /       \
   9.75 — ☐ — 5.75
```

Maths Test A

10 Playing cards come in different suits.

diamonds   clubs   spades   hearts

Here are five playing cards.

These five cards are shuffled and spread out face down on a table. **One card** is picked from them.

a What is the probability that it is a **heart**? Give your answer as a fraction.

b What is the probability that it is a **diamond**? Show your answer by drawing a cross on this line.

0 ———————————————— 1

11 The hundreds digits are missing from two numbers in this number sentence. Write what they could be.

☐ 5 9 + ☐ 7 4 = 833

Maths Test A

12 Look at this multiplication fact.

$$26 \times 123 = 3198$$

Use this fact to find the answers to these questions:

a $25 \times 123 = $ ☐

b $26 \times 124 = $ ☐

c $260 \times 123 = $ ☐

d $2.6 \times 12.3 = $ ☐

13 Circle **two** fractions below that are equivalent.

$\dfrac{2}{5}$ $\dfrac{3}{8}$ $\dfrac{6}{10}$ $\dfrac{6}{16}$

$\dfrac{6}{12}$ $\dfrac{1}{10}$ $\dfrac{6}{8}$

14 Calculate **952 − 436** ☐

Maths Test A

15 a Using a ruler, and a mirror or tracing paper, **draw and shade** the reflection of the shape below in the mirror line.

b What area of the grid is now shaded? ☐ cm²

c What fraction of the grid is now shaded? ☐

d How many degrees is **angle a**? You may use an angle measurer (protractor). ☐

16 Here are two squares drawn on a graph.
Fill in the missing **co-ordinates** of **point C**.

A (12, 10)
B (3, 4)
C (,)

TOTAL 7

17 In a gymnastics competition, the gymnasts are awarded points for **difficulty**, **style** and **technical merit**. These points are added together to find a total score.

Here are the numbers of points awarded to three children.

Name	Difficulty	Style	Technical merit
Alice	3.8	5.1	4.7
Ajay	4.3	4.9	5.2
Emily	5.4	4.6	4.8

a What is the **total** number of points awarded for **style**?

b Which of Ajay's marks was closest to 5 points?

c Whose total score was 14.8?

Maths Test A

18 Mrs Wood is buying some fruit.

The fruit comes in bags of different sizes. This table shows the prices of the different bags.

	Bananas	Apples
500 g	69p	35p
750 g	99p	50p
1 kg	£1.25	65p

Mrs Wood buys **three bags** of fruit. She buys **one** 500 g bag, **one** 750 g bag and **one** 1 kg bag.

a What is the total **mass** of fruit she buys?

b She spends a total of **£2.33**.

Which **three** bags of fruit does she buy?

500 g   750 g   1 kg

STOP HERE AND MARK THE TEST

Maths Test
Test B (with calculator)

1 Write three numbers to make the number sentence correct.

☐ + ☐ + ☐ = 104

2 An arrow is pointing to each of the number lines below.
Write the numbers indicated by the arrows in the boxes.

a
0 — 100

b
400 — 600

c
2500 — 3500

3 Here are some number riddles.
Write the number for each riddle in the box.

a
The number is less than 40.
It is a multiple of 6.
It is a multiple of 4.
It is a multiple of 9.

b
The number is between 30 and 50.
It is a square number.
It is an odd number.

TOTAL 6

Maths Test B

4 Write what the **missing numbers** could be to make the number sentences correct.

a ☐ – ☐ + ☐ = 25

b ☐ ÷ ☐ = 8

c 5 × 3 + ☐ = 6 × ☐

5 On Sunday **£4416** was paid by people entering a theme park. They each paid **£12** to get in.

a How many people went to the theme park on Sunday?

Ice creams cost 75p each.
A **total** of **253** ice creams were bought.

b How much money was spent on ice creams in total?

Maths Test B

6 This diagram shows the **number of kilometres** between some cities in the United Kingdom.

	Aberdeen	Bristol	Glasgow	Manchester	Dover
Aberdeen	—	490	150	332	574
Bristol	490	—	366	167	195
Glasgow	150	366	—	210	467
Manchester	332	167	210	—	265
Dover	574	195	467	265	—

a Explain why each number appears twice in the table.

_____
_____
_____

1

b A delivery driver visits three cities on the same journey. She starts at **Bristol**, drives to **Manchester** and then on to **Dover**. How far does she travel?

[km   ]

2

7 Use all of these digits to make the four-digit number closest to 5000.

| 8 | 4 | 3 | 5 |

[   ]

1

TOTAL

4

13

Maths Test B

8 Here is an arrangement of dots. Join some of these dots with straight lines to draw a **regular hexagon**. Use a ruler.

9 Hannah is colouring a flag.

The pattern she is colouring has **rotational symmetry**.

She still has **one square** to colour.

Shade **one** square so that the pattern will have **rotational symmetry**.

10 This number sequence is made by counting on in steps of **equal size**. Fill in the **missing numbers**.

| 4 | | | 22 | |

14

Maths Test B

11 David is playing a game using a set of ten **different** number cards showing **1 to 10**. He turns over two cards and adds the numbers to find the **total**.

These are his first four goes:

Card 1	Card 2	Total
6	7	13
3	5	8
4	9	13
7	2	9

a What is the **lowest total** David could possibly get?

b Jenny says,
"You are equally likely to get a total of 10 as a total of 3."
Is she correct?
Circle yes or no.

yes | no

Explain your answer.

_____

_____

12 Fill in the missing numbers to make these statements correct.

a 53 912 ÷ ☐ = 586

b 5748 × ☐ = 120 708

13 Look carefully at the shapes below.

Square — A
Trapezium — B
Isosceles triangle — C
Regular octagon — D

Write the letter of shapes **B**, **C** and **D** into the correct section of the table below. **A** has been done for you.

	No pairs of parallel sides	One pair of parallel sides	More than one pair of parallel sides
3 sides			
4 sides			A
More than 4 sides			

14 Calculate 32% of 950.

15 Mr Hall is making some blackcurrant drink.

He uses **125 ml** of blackcurrant squash and then fills the jug to the top with water.

a Use a ruler to draw a **line** to show where the **125 ml** of blackcurrant squash would come to on the **litre** container.

b How many times more water than blackcurrant squash does Mr Hall use?

c Mr Hall drinks **one-quarter** of the litre of blackcurrant drink. How much drink does he have now?

Give your answer in **litres**.

Maths Test B

16 Carol is arranging exactly **four** number cards to make different fractions **less than one**. These are the numbers.

10   2   5   4

a Using **each** number card only **once**, show where each would go to make this statement correct.

☐/☐ is the same value as ☐/☐

b Find another way to place these cards to make **different** fractions that have the same value.

☐/☐ is the same value as ☐/☐

17 Here is part of a flower bed.

Each flower bed has **342** daffodils. Each row has **19** daffodils in it. How many rows of daffodils are in **8** flower beds?

18 Jack and Chloe go to a car boot sale. They buy some books.

Entrance fee 75p and 20p for each book

a Jack pays the **entrance fee** and buys **twelve books**.

How much does he spend?

b Chloe pays the **entrance fee** and buys some books.

She spends exactly **£2.55**.

How many books does she buy?

Entrance fee 75p and 20p for each book

c Write a formula to show the total cost (**C**) in pence of visiting the car boot sale if you buy **n** books.

C =

STOP HERE AND MARK THE TEST

Mental Maths Test
Questions

"For this first set of questions you have five seconds to work out each answer and write it down."

1 Write the number four thousand and nine in figures.

2 What is twenty-two less than forty?

3 What is twice one point seven?

4 Seven-tenths of the children in a class are boys. What percentage are boys?

5 How many sides do three octagons have in total?

6 What is half of seventy-two?

"For the next set of questions you have ten seconds to work out each answer and write it down."

7 What is double one hundred and eighty?

8 How many minutes are there in two and a half hours?

9 Add five and nineteen and then divide by three.

10 A snail crawls eighty-one centimetres. How much further does it have to crawl to reach one metre?

11 Twenty per cent of a number is thirty. What is the number?

12 On the answer sheet is part of a scale. What number is the arrow pointing to?

13 A shop has a sale. All items are twenty-five per cent of their original price. A video costs four pounds in the sale. What was its original price?

14 Sam cycles six miles every day. How far does he cycle in a week?

15 Look at the answer sheet. Draw a ring around the approximate height of a door.

"For the next set of questions you have fifteen seconds to work out each answer and write it down."

16 Look at the answer sheet. Draw a ring around the number that is nearest to seven.

17 Two-fifths of a number is twelve. What is the number?

18 Which year is seventeen years before the year two thousand and two?

19 Look at the answer sheet. What is the size of angle A?

20 Look at the answer sheet. Draw a ring around three numbers that are multiples of twenty.

Mental Maths Test
Answer Sheet

5-second questions

1 ☐
2 ☐
3 ☐
4 ☐
5 ☐
6 ☐

6

10-second questions

7 ☐

8 ☐ minutes

9 ☐

10 ☐ centimetres

11 ☐

12 ☐ [scale from 4.6 to 4.7 with arrow]

13 £ ☐

14 ☐ miles

15 2000 cm   20 m
    200 cm
    20 cm   2 cm

9

15-second questions

16 0.7   7.9   6.6
    7.5   7.74

17 ☐

18 ☐

19 A= [triangle with 90°, 50°, and A angles]

20 240   130   290
    88   580   200

5

TOTAL

20

21

Answers
Maths Test

Question number	Answer	Mark	Parent's notes and additional information
TEST A			
1a	6	1	
1b	11	1	
1c	e.g. 10, 20	1	Two numbers to make the equation true.
2	20, 30	1	
3a	15, 21	1	
3b	A mark for either: an explanation that the differences between numbers in the sequence go up in ones *or* a reference to counting on, e.g. "one number missed out, two numbers missed out, etc."	1	Children's answers to questions like these should include <u>numbers</u> to support their explanations. Just writing "I saw a pattern. The numbers go up" is generally not enough to score a mark.
4	112 ÷ 7 = 16	2	It does not matter whether this calculation is done mentally or using a written method. One mark for an attempt to divide 112 by 7.
5	Any three <u>different</u> numbers that have a total of 27, e.g. 8, 9, 10 or 20, 3, 4.	1	The mean (average) of a set of numbers is found by finding the total and dividing this by the number of numbers in the set. In this case there are 3 numbers so the mean is **27 ÷ 3 = 9**.
6a	34	1	Children are required to interpret the table and then find the total of 14, 12 and 8.
6b	vanilla	1	Children should check the total of each row to find the flavour that adds to 31.
7	Any shape with more than 4 sides and with exactly 3 right angles. External right angles (those outside the shape) do not count.	2	Examples of shapes: One mark if the shape has more than 4 sides and some right angles.
8a	£8.50 Note that amounts of money should never be written with both the **£** sign and a **p** sign, e.g. £8.50p is incorrect and would not earn a mark.	1	Children must double £4.25. Children of this age should try to learn doubles of all numbers to 100 and their corresponding halves, e.g. double 25 = 50 and half of 50 = 25. They can then use this knowledge for questions of this kind.
8b	£7.25	1	
9	Any 3 numbers that make the sides add to same total, e.g. 2.25 at left, 4.25 at right, 1 at base (total 16.5)	2	All three sides should have the same total.
10a	$\frac{1}{5}$	1	There are 5 cards. The probability of picking the only heart is one out of five. Probabilities generally can be written in words or as fractions or decimals, e.g. **one out of five**, $\frac{1}{5}$ or **0.20**.
10b		1	There are 5 cards. The probability of picking one of the two diamonds is two out of five = 0.40.
11	Two digits that add to make 7, e.g. **159 + 674** **259 + 574** **359 + 474** **459 + 374** **559 + 274** or **659 + 174**	1	If your child has written two digits that add to make 8, encourage him or her to add the two numbers together, e.g. 459 + 474 Point out that the answer comes to 933.
12a	3075	1	Your child should notice that 25 × 123 is 123 less than 26 × 123. Ideally he or she should subtract 123 from 3198 to get 3075. A mark can be awarded if the answer was found using a different method.
12b	3224	1	Again, your child should notice that 26 × 124 is 26 more than 26 × 123. If he or she finds this difficult, discuss it in a context, e.g. 124 things costing £26, cost £26 more than 123 things costing £26.

Maths Test Answers

Question number	Answer	Mark	Parent's notes and additional information
12c	31 980	1	This answer is ten times larger than the given multiplication fact.
12d	31.98	1	Encourage your child to work out an approximate answer to decide where the decimal point should go, e.g. **2.6** × **12.3** is approximately **3** × **12** = 36, so the answer is not 319.8 or 3.198, but 31.98.
13	$\frac{3}{8}$ and $\frac{6}{16}$ are equivalent.	1	Equivalent means that the fractions have the same value, e.g. if you have $\frac{3}{8}$ of a pizza it is the same value as $\frac{6}{16}$ of a pizza.
14	516	1	
15a		2	Award one mark if 5 or 6 out of the 7 corners of the shape are reflected correctly.
15b	16 cm^2	1	The area of a shape is the number of whole squares inside the shape. In this case it is centimetre squares or cm^2 that are counted. If your child gave the answer 22, he or she counted half squares as whole squares.
15c	$\frac{16}{40}$ or $\frac{8}{20}$ or $\frac{4}{10}$ or $\frac{2}{5}$	1	There should be 16 out of 40 squares shaded.
15d	45° Accept answers that are 1 degree either side of 45°, i.e. 44° or 46°.	1	A protractor is not essential for this question. Show your child that the angle is half a right angle and that the exact answer is 90 ÷ 2 = 45°.
16	(21, 4)	2	Award one mark for each co-ordinate. The second co-ordinate (how many up) is the same as B, i.e. 4. To work out the first co-ordinate (how far across) find the difference between 3 and 12 = 9 and then add this to 12 to get 21.
17a	14.6	1	5.1 + 4.9 + 4.6
17b	4.9 (for style)	1	Children may incorrectly answer 5.2. Show that 5.2 is two-tenths away from 5 whereas 4.9 is one-tenth away from 5.
17c	Emily	2	3.8 + 5.1 + 4.7 = 13.6 4.3 + 4.9 + 5.2 = 14.4 5.4 + 4.6 + 4.8 = 14.8 Award one mark for workings that show some correct addition of scores.
18a	2250 g or 2.25 kg	1	500 g + 750 g + 1 kg (1000 g)
18b	500 g bananas (69p), 750 g bananas (99p), 1 kg apples (65p).	2	This question involves interpreting information and dealing with two criteria: the price (£2.33) and the different masses of the bags. Award one mark for attempts to add sets of three numbers, including prices and masses.
TEST B			
1	Any three numbers that add to make 104.	1	
2a	70	1	Show your child that the 100 is split into 10 sections, so each must be worth 10.
2b	560	1	Show your child that the 200 is split into 10 sections, so each must be worth 20.
2c	2800	1	Show your child that the 1000 is split into 10 sections, so each must be worth 100.
3a	36	1	A multiple is a number that can be divided exactly into without a remainder, e.g. multiples of 6 include 6, 12, 18, 180, 486, etc.
3b	49	1	A square number is a number that is made from multiplying another number by itself, e.g. 4 = 2 × 2, 9 = 3 × 3, 25 = 5 × 5. Children should learn the square numbers to 100, i.e. 1, 4, 9, 16, 25, 36, 49, 64, 81, 100.

23

Maths Test Answers

Question number	Answer	Mark	Parent's notes and additional information
4a	Any three numbers that make 25, e.g. 50 − 30 + 5, 100 − 80 + 5.	1	
4b	Any numbers that divide to make 8, e.g. 8 ÷ 1, 16 ÷ 2, 24 ÷ 3, 80 ÷ 10.	1	
4c	Any numbers that make the statement correct, e.g. 5 × 3 + **3** = 6 × **3** 5 × 3 + **9** = 6 × **4** 5 × 3 + **15** = 6 × **5**.	1	Children often find this type of question difficult as they see the equals sign as an "answer giver" rather than meaning "is/has the same answer as". Here 5 × 3 + ☐ "has the same answer as" 6 × ☐. Also, 5 × 3 must be multiplied before adding the missing number.
5a	368	1	4416 ÷ 12
5b	£189.75	2	Here children must be aware of their actions if they multiply by 0.75 or 75. If they multiply by 0.75 their answer will be in pounds but if they multiply by 75 their answer will be in pence so they will need to divide by 100.
6a	Any explanation showing that your child appreciates that the distance between two towns, e.g. Bristol to Dover, will be the same distance in reverse, e.g. Dover to Bristol.	1	
6b	432 km	2	A common mistake is to select the incorrect second distance. If your child answered 362 km, it is because he or she used the distances between Bristol and Manchester (167) and then between <u>Bristol</u> and Dover (195), rather than Bristol and Manchester (167) and on from <u>Manchester</u> to Dover (265). Award one mark if the working shows 167 + 265, but with an incorrect answer.
7	4853	1	
8	A regular hexagon has 6 equal sides and 6 equal angles.	1	
9		1	Shapes or patterns that have rotational symmetry can look the same in more than one orientation when turned. Letters like S, H, X, O have rotational symmetry, but A, E, T, W do not. They cannot be turned to look the same in any other orientation.
10	10, 16, 28	1	To answer this question, your child should find the difference between 22 and 4 = 18. If the difference between boxes that are three apart is 18 then the difference between each box is 18 ÷ 3 = 6.
11a	3	1	David can pick a 1 and a 2 card, with a total of 3.
11b	no There must be an explanation with reference to the fact that there are more ways to make 10 than there are to make 3, e.g. 3 can only be scored with a 1 and a 2 card, whereas 10 can be scored with a 1 and 9, 2 and 8, 3 and 7, 6 and 4, etc.	1	Children's answers to questions like these should include <u>numbers</u>, where possible. It is not enough to say that "it is more likely to score 10 than 3".
12a	92	1	Children often attempt questions of this type using trial and error, e.g. trying to divide 53 912 by different numbers to get 586. This involves a great deal of time. Instead, encourage your child to see that division questions can be rearranged, e.g. 10 ÷ 5 = 2 and 10 ÷ 2 = 5. Here children should divide 53 912 by 586 to get 92.
12b	21	1	Again, children attempt questions of this type using trial and error, e.g. trying to multiply 5748 by different numbers to get 12 0708. Instead, encourage your child to see that multiplication questions can be rearranged, e.g. 2 × 5 = 10 can be rearranged to make 10 ÷ 2 = 5. Here children should divide 12 0708 by 5748 to get 21.

Maths Test Answers

Question number	Answer	Mark	Parent's notes and additional information
13	(grid with C top-left of centre, B middle-left of centre, A middle-right, D bottom-right)	3	Parallel lines are lines that if extended in either direction would never meet. Parallel lines are the same distance apart. A regular shape has equal sides and equal angles. Award one mark for each of the letters B, C and D correctly positioned.
14	304	1	32% of 950 can be worked out in the following ways: 32 ÷ 100 × 950 or 32 × 950 ÷ 100 or 0.32 × 950
15a	(jug showing 125 ml marked)	1	Show children that the litre jug (1000 ml) is split into 10 sections, so each must be worth 100, so 125 will come a quarter of the way between 100 and 200.
15b	7	2	Marks are awarded for the correct answer, whatever the method. Award one mark if the working shows an attempt to subtract 125 ml from 1 litre and divide by 125, but with an incorrect answer.
15c	0.75 l	1	
16a	$\frac{4}{10}$ and $\frac{2}{5}$ or $\frac{2}{4}$ and $\frac{5}{10}$	1	The fractions can be in any order, e.g. $\frac{2}{5}$ and $\frac{4}{10}$ or $\frac{4}{10}$ and $\frac{2}{5}$
16b	$\frac{4}{10}$ and $\frac{2}{5}$ or $\frac{2}{4}$ and $\frac{5}{10}$	1	Do not award a mark if the answer has the same fractions as question 16a, even if given in a different order.
17	144	2	Award one mark for a method that shows 342 ÷ 19 × 8, but with an incorrect answer.
18a	£3.15 Do not award a mark for the answer £3.15p or £315.	1	Money answers must be written correctly for questions of this type. Calculator questions like these are often selected to see whether children can interpret the display in the context of money. Amounts of money should never be written with both the £ sign and a p sign.
18b	9	2	Children may incorrectly answer 12.75 or 13. Remind them that the entrance fee (75p) should be subtracted first. Award one mark for attempts to subtract 75 from 255 and divide this by 20.
18c	Any of the following answers: C = 75 + (20 × n) C = 75 + (n × 20) C = 75 + 20n C = 20n + 75 C = 20 × n + 75 etc. Award one mark for C = 20n or C = 20 × n	2	Children find using letters in place of numbers quite difficult. Show them the following: For 1 book C (cost) = 75 + (1 × 20) For 2 books C (cost) = 75 + (2 × 20) For 3 books C (cost) = 75 + (3 × 20), etc. So for n books C (cost) = 75 + (n × 20).

Answers
Mental Maths Test

1. 4009
2. 18
3. 3.4
4. 70%
5. 24
6. 36
7. 360
8. 150 minutes
9. 8
10. 19 cm
11. 150
12. 4.67
13. £16
14. 42 miles
15. 200 cm
16. 6.6
17. 30
18. 1985
19. 40°
20. 240, 580, 200

One mark per correct answer.

25

National Curriculum Levels
Maths

Write your child's scores in the Maths Tests below.

Mark scored in Test A [   ] out of 40

Mark scored in Test B [   ] out of 40

Mark scored in Mental Maths Test [   ] out of 20

Total score [   ] out of 100

The National Tests are levelled according to the child's total score.

Mark	0–24	25–51	52–79	80–100
Level	1/2	3	4	5

For each test this can be broadly broken down as follows:

TEST A	Mark	0–10	11–20	21–31	32–40
	Level	1/2	3	4	5

TEST B	Mark	0–10	11–20	21–31	32–40
	Level	1/2	3	4	5

MENTAL TEST	Mark	0–4	5–10	11–15	16–20
	Level	1/2	3	4	5

If your child needs more practice in any Maths topics, use the WHSmith Key Stage 2 Maths Revision Guide.

English Test

Reading Test

The Reading Test at Key Stage 2 comprises a variety of texts – non-fiction, fiction and poetry – to test reading strategies across a range of genres. There will normally be a common theme.

The questions require four different kinds of answers:
- Short words or phrases (one mark for each correct response).
- Longer answers (one or two sentences) which require more understanding of the text (two marks).
- Detailed explanations of opinion (up to three marks).
- Multiple choice (one mark).

Although some questions will have a "right answer", all children will express their responses in a different way. Marking guidelines are given on page 49 and an indication of National Curriculum Levels on page 51.

Setting the test

Allow 15 minutes for reading the passages (when no writing is allowed) and 45 minutes for answering the questions.

1. Encourage your child to read the introduction on the next page and each passage carefully.
2. Point out the different types of questions: those which give a choice of answers to tick and those which need a written answer. Written answers need not be complete sentences. Some written answers are worth three or more marks if detail or examples are required.
3. Do not help your child to read the text, although you may help with the spelling of the answers.
4. Point out that your child may rub out or alter any mistakes.
5. Tell your child:
   - to find the answers in the text, rather than guessing;
   - to tick only one box in multiple choice questions;
   - to try to answer every question;
   - to leave any questions he or she cannot answer and go back to them at the end;
   - to re-read the text to find the answers.

Reading Test

Different views of Christmas

Contents

Non-fiction: **Christmas Celebrations**

Fiction: **Christmas Eve**

Poetry: **A Week to Christmas**

Christmas means different things to different people.

In these extracts, we look at different people's experiences and views of Christmas:

- from an information text about what Christmas means to Christians (a website to which people from different countries sent information);

- from a novel set about 130 years ago;

- from a twentieth-century poem.

You have **15 minutes** to read through these three passages, and **45 minutes** to answer the questions.

Christmas Celebrations

People around the world celebrate Christmas in different ways, both religious and non-religious. Many celebrations are based on legends and traditions which pre-date Christianity, and important dates in the Christian calendar (such as Epiphany, on 6 January) are sometimes linked with the dates of pagan festivals. Many celebrations include the traditional foods of a country and many are influenced by the climate of the country.

Mexico

As Christmas approaches, elaborately decorated market stalls are set up in town centres to sell crafts, foods such as cheese, bananas, nuts and cookies, and flowers such as orchids and poinsettias.

There is a legend about the poinsettia. A little boy gathered some green branches from along the roadside while he was walking to church to look at the Nativity scene (the birth of Jesus). Other children laughed when he laid them by the manger as an offering, but they fell silent when a brilliant red, star-shaped flower appeared on each branch.

Processions which enact Joseph and Mary's search for somewhere to stay in Bethlehem on the night Jesus was born begin nine days before Christmas, because Mary and Joseph's journey from Nazareth to Bethlehem took nine days. People form two groups: pilgrims and innkeepers. The pilgrims trudge from house to house asking for shelter. The innkeepers turn them away until they reach the house in which an altar and Nativity scene have been set up. They go in with great rejoicing, a traditional prayer is spoken, and the party begins.

Sweden

The "Yule log" comes from Scandinavia. Traditions concerned with warmth and light arose because of the long, dark, cold winters. Yuletide means "the turning of the sun" (the winter solstice). It was traditionally a time when fortunes for the coming year were determined and when the dead were thought to walk the earth.

Originally an entire tree was brought into the house with great ceremony. The bottom of the trunk was set into the hearth so that the rest of the tree stuck out into the room. It was burned until 6 January (the end of Yule).

A thousand years ago in Sweden, the King declared that Christmas would last a month, from the Feast of Saint Lucia (13 December) until Saint Knut's Day (13 January). Lucia was a 4th-century Sicilian saint and martyr who took food to Christians hiding from persecution in dark underground tunnels. To light the way she wore a wreath of candles on her head. She was discovered and killed. It is not known why she came to be revered in Sweden. Schools, businesses and communities sponsor processions of girls wearing white dresses and wreaths of candles; carols are sung and the Queen of Light is thanked for bringing hope at the darkest time of the year.

On Christmas Eve a Christmas gnome emerges from his home under the floor of the house or the barn. He brings a sack of gifts.

Nicaragua

In Nicaragua, Christmas begins on 7 December with *La Griteria* (The Calling), when groups of people call at each house in the neighbourhood singing joyful hymns to the Virgin Mary. The singers are given sweets and other small gifts. A giant doll, *La Gigantona* (The Female Giant), a symbol of Mary, is paraded dancing through the streets to the accompaniment of drums.

Reading Test

Japan
Christmas became popular in Japan at the beginning of the 20th century because of the Christmas products made there for other countries. It is a non-religious holiday devoted to children, and is celebrated mainly in cities.

Tinsel and lights are hung in dance halls, cafés and pinball parlours. Trees are decorated with small toys, dolls, gold paper fans and lanterns, wind chimes, candles and paper ornaments including origami swans.

Japanese children call Santa "Santa Kuroshu". He is believed to have eyes in the back of his head – to watch the children all year long!

Jamaica
On Christmas morning, processions of *jonkonoo* (masked dancing men) parade down the streets, beating drums to herald Christmas Day.

Ghana
In Ghana, Christmas celebrations go on for eight days. Children are given new clothes and other gifts. Bells ring all morning to call people to church.

The main dish for Christmas Day dinner is usually made from a fowl, goat or sheep. Yams and a soup made of meat and eggs are served.

In most towns, groups of children go from house to house, singing or chanting and blowing home-made trumpets throughout the eight days.

Iceland
Icelandic tradition has thirteen *Jolasveinar* (Christmas elves). Jolasveinar first appeared in the 17th century – the sons of the ogres Gryla and Leppaludi, who themselves had appeared in the 13th century and were said to have stolen and eaten naughty children.

The Jolasveinar live in mountains and start to arrive in towns, one a day, thirteen days before Christmas Eve, with the last one arriving that morning. As their names suggest, the Jolasveinar are playful imps who steal the seasonal food and play tricks: Door Slammer awakens sleepers by slamming doors; Candle Beggar snatches candles; and Meat Hooker tries to run off with the roast.

They also leave presents for children (in shoes the children have left on the windowsill the night before). If any children have been naughty, they leave a potato or some other reminder to be good. They start departing for home on Christmas Day, with the last one departing on Twelfth Night (6 January).

Reading Test

1 In which four countries are there special Christmas processions?

_____

_____

[2]

2 Which of the processions are linked with the Nativity?

_____

_____

[2]

What tells you this?

_____

_____

_____

_____

[2]

3 Which country's Christmas celebrations have arisen because of the weather or climate there?

_____

[1]

4 Give three examples of Christmas celebrations which are based on legends not connected with the Nativity.

_____

_____

_____

_____

[3]

TOTAL 10

Reading Test

5 What is the main similarity between Christmas celebrations in Sweden and Iceland?

_____
_____
_____

6 Japan is not a Christian country. What made the Japanese begin to celebrate Christmas?

_____
_____
_____

7 In which two countries are children likely to make sure they behave themselves as Christmas approaches?

_____
_____

Explain your answer.

_____
_____
_____
_____
_____

8 In which country does the Christmas season begin the earliest?

_____

9 In Sweden, what is the link between Saint Lucia and yuletide festivals?

_____
_____
_____
_____
_____

10 Which traditional festivals, in which countries, are linked with the date of the Christian festival of Epiphany?

_____
_____
_____
_____

Reading Test
Fiction

Christmas Eve
From *Her Benny* by Silas Hocking

This book is set in Liverpool in the 1870s. Benny is ten and Nelly is nine years old. They make a living by selling matches. Benny also carries people's bags to and from the ferry-boats.

On Christmas Eve Benny took his sister through St John's Market, and highly delighted they were with what they saw. The thousands of geese, turkeys and pheasants, the loads of vegetables, the heaps of oranges and apples, the pyramids of every other conceivable kind of fruit, the stalls of sweetmeats, the tons of toffee, and the crowds of well-dressed people all bent upon buying something, were sources of infinite pleasure to the children. There was only one drawback to their happiness – they did not know how to lay out the sixpence they had brought with them to spend. If there had been less variety there would have been less difficulty; but, as it was, Benny felt as if he would never be able to decide what to buy. However, they agreed at last to lay out twopence for two slices of bread and ham, for they were both rather hungry; and then they spent the other fourpence on apples, oranges and toffee and, on the whole, felt very well satisfied with the result of their outlay.

It was rather later than usual when they got home, but old Betty knew where they had gone and, as it was Christmas Eve, she had got a bigger fire in than usual and had also got them a cup of hot cocoa each and some bunloaf to eat with it.

"By golly!" said Benny, as he munched the cake, "I do wish folks 'ud 'ave Christmas ev'ry week."

"You are a curious boy," said the old woman, looking up with a smile on her wrinkled face.

"Is I, Granny? I specks it's in my blood, as the chap said o' his timber leg."

The old woman had told them on the first evening of their arrival, when they had seemed at a loss what name to give her, to call her "Granny"; and no name could have been more appropriate, or have come more readily to the children's lips.

"But could folks 'ave Christmas any oftener if they wished to?" asked little Nell.

"Of course they could, Nell," burst out Benny. "You dunna seem to know what folks make Christmas for."

"An' I thinks you dunno either, Benny."

"Don't I, though?" he said, putting on an air of importance. "It's made to give folks the chance of doing a lot o' feeding; didn't yer see all the gooses an' other nice things in the market that folks is going to polish off tomorrow?"

"I dunna think it was made purpose for that. Wur it now, Granny?"

Reading Test

Thus appealed to, the old woman, who had listened with an amused smile on her face, answered, "No, my child. It's called Christmas because it is the birthday of Christ."

"Who's he?" said Benny, looking up, while Nelly's eyes echoed the enquiry.

"Don't you know – ain't you never heerd?" said the old woman in a tone of surprise.

"Nay," said Benny, "nuthin' sense."

"Poor little dears! I didn't know as how you was so ignorant, or I should have told you before." And the old woman looked as if she did not know where or how to begin to tell the children the wonderful story, and for a considerable time remained silent. At length she said, "I'll read it to 'ee out o' the Book; mebbe you'll understand it better that way nor any way else."

And, taking down from a shelf her big and much-worn Bible, she opened it and began to read:

"Now when Jesus was born in Bethlehem of Judea …" And slowly the old woman read on until she reached the end of the chapter, while the children listened with wide and wondering eyes. To Nelly the words seemed like a revelation, responding to the deepest feeling in her nature, and awakening thoughts within her that were too big for utterance. Benny, however, could see nothing particularly interesting in the narrative itself. But the art of reading was to him a mystery past all comprehension. How Granny could see that story upon the pages of her Bible was altogether beyond his grasp. At length, after scratching his head vigorously for some time, he burst out:

"By jabbers! I's got it at last! Jimmy Jones squeeze me if I ain't! It's the specks that does it!"

"Does what?" said Nelly.

"Why, the story bizness, to be sure. Let me look at the book through your specks, shall I, Granny?"

"Ay, if you like, Benny." And the next minute he was looking at the Bible with Granny's spectacles astride his nose and an expression of disappointment upon his face.

"Golly! I's sold!" was his exclamation. "But this are a poser, and no mistake."

"What's such a poser?" said Granny.

"Why, how yer find the story in the book; for I can see nowt."

Reading Test

Tick the correct answer for questions 1–6.

1 What made it difficult for the children to spend their sixpence?

| everything cost more than sixpence | they had to hurry because it was late | there was too much choice | they didn't see anything they wanted |

2 Who was old Betty?

| the children's grandmother | the person they lived with | their mother | their neighbour |

3 What impressed Benny most about Christmas?

| the food | it was Christ's birthday | the snow | the money people spent |

4 What surprised old Betty?

| the amount of food the children ate | they had money to spend | they were late coming home | they didn't know who Christ was |

5 Why was Betty silent for quite a long time?

| she didn't know how or where to begin telling them the story of Christ | she was speechless at their ignorance | the children were arguing about what Christmas was for | she was day-dreaming |

6 What does Benny mean by "I specks"?

| a pair of glasses | the text on a page | I expect | my place |

36

Reading Test

7 Do you think the children go to school?

_____

How can you tell?

_____
_____

8 List three different exclamations of surprise used by Benny.

_____
_____
_____

9 What does Benny mean by "Jimmy Jones squeeze me if I ain't"?

_____
_____
_____
_____

10 From the dialogue, give:

four examples in which verbs and pronouns do not agree

_____   _____

_____   _____

a non-standard plural _____
a non-standard past tense _____
a double negative _____

1

1

3

1

2

3

TOTAL

11

37

Reading Test

11 List four dialect words (other than exclamations) which the characters use, and their meanings.

_____
_____
_____
_____

12 What was the atmosphere of St John's Market like?

_____

How does the author create this atmosphere?

_____
_____
_____

13 Give three examples of alliteration in the description of the market.

_____
_____
_____

14 What was the main difference between the responses of Benny and Nell to the story?

_____
_____
_____
_____

2

1

1

2

2

TOTAL

8

38

15 How does the author help the reader to imagine the characters' accents?

_____

_____

Give four examples.

_____   _____

_____   _____

16 What can you tell about the narrator's religious beliefs?

_____

How can you tell?

_____

_____

_____

_____

_____

Reading Test
Poetry

A Week to Christmas

Sunday with six whole days to go
How we'll endure it I don't know!

Monday the goodies are in the making,
Spice smells of pudding and mince pies a-baking.

Tuesday, Dad's home late and quiet as a mouse
He smuggles packages into the house.

Wednesday's the day for decorating the tree,
Will the lights work again? We'll have to see!

Thursday's for last minute shopping and hurry,
We've never seen Mum in quite such a flurry!

Friday is Christmas Eve when we'll lie awake
Trying to sleep before the day break.

And that special quiet of Christmas morn
When out there somewhere Christ was born.

John Cotton

Reading Test

1 How many days before Christmas does the poem begin?

   _____

2 Name four Christmas foods or decorations which are mentioned in the poem.

   _____   _____

   _____   _____

3 List four ways in which the family prepares for Christmas.

   _____

   _____

   _____

   _____

4 Which line suggests a slight worry about a possible problem?

   _____

   _____

5 Who is panicking a little?

   _____

   How can you tell?

   _____

Reading Test

6 Which three separate lines suggest excitement?

_____
_____
_____

Which punctuation mark helps to create this effect?

_____

7 Which verse has a much calmer atmosphere than the others?

_____

In what other way is this verse different from the others?

_____
_____
_____
_____

Writing Test

This test helps you to gain an insight into your child's ability to write independently and to communicate meaning to the reader using the conventions of punctuation, spelling and handwriting.

At Key Stage 2 children's writing is assessed through two Writing Tests:

- a Longer Writing Test (45 minutes)
- a Shorter Writing Test (20 minutes).

Children should be allowed time to plan their writing for both tests, which they should not do one after the other.

In the National Tests, the **Longer Test** is assessed for: **Sentence structure and punctuation**, **Text structure and organisation** and **Composition and effect**. The **Shorter Test** is assessed for **Sentence structure, punctuation and text organisation** and **Composition and effect**.

Sentence structure and punctuation focuses on the use of variation of types of sentences, clarity, purpose and effect, and on grammatical accuracy and punctuation.

Text structure and organisation focuses on organising and presenting whole texts effectively, sequencing and structuring information, ideas and events, constructing paragraphs and using cohesion within and between paragraphs.

Composition and effect focuses on imaginative, interesting and thoughtful writing; writing a text which is suitable for its purpose and for the reader; and organising and presenting a text effectively.

Handwriting is assessed within the Longer Test, but is not assessed in this book.

Spelling is assessed in a separate test.

The mark schemes each year are specific to the tests; new level thresholds are set for each year's tests to ensure that standards are maintained each year.

Assessment of children's attainment in National Tests depends on the judgement of professionals who use a more precise numerical marking system. For the purposes of this book, a simplified system of marking is used based on Content (Composition and effect) and Grammar and structure (Sentence structure, Punctuation and Text organisation).

Guidelines to National Curriculum Levels are provided on page 50. These should be regarded as a rough guide only.

Writing Test

Your child should first have read the passages in the Reading Tests.

Allow **45 minutes** for the **Longer (Fiction)** Writing Test and **20 minutes** for the **Shorter (Non-fiction)** Writing Test.

There are no definitive answers, but criteria are given on page 50 to help you assess your child's National Curriculum Level.

FOR NON-FICTION: Discuss the points on the planning sheet. Emphasise the importance of:

- thinking up a good introduction to make the reader want to read on;
- keeping the reader interested;
- making the text easy for the reader to follow;
- thinking of a good ending so that the information does not just "tail off".

You must not tell your child what to write!

FOR FICTION: Introduce the planning sheet and read the starting point aloud. Discuss the headings on the sheet. Emphasise the importance of:

- writing a whole story and not just part of it;
- planning the story;
- thinking of a good opening to make the reader want to read on;
- keeping the reader interested;
- introducing the setting, the main character and the plot early in the story;
- helping the reader to get to know the characters;
- thinking of a good ending, rather than stopping abruptly.

For both tasks, point out that grammar, spelling and punctuation are important.

Remind your child to think about punctuation and how it helps the reader to make sense of what is written.

If your child finishes before the allotted time is up, encourage him or her to read through what he or she has written to look for anything which can be improved and to check grammar, spelling and punctuation.

Longer Writing Test (Fiction)
Planning Sheet

Making sense of Christmas

Read the extract from *Her Benny* and the poem "A Week to Christmas". Write a story from the point of view of a visitor from another planet who has observed people celebrating Christmas and is trying to make sense of what he or she observes.

You have 45 minutes. Spend about 10 to 15 minutes of this time planning what you will write. Use the planning guidelines below.

Title

Setting
Where does the story take place?

When does it take place?

Characters
Name them and make notes about their personal qualities and characteristics.

Who is the main character or the narrator?

Who are the other characters?

Opening
Think of an opening which sets the scene and interests the reader.

Middle
Plan this section in paragraphs: what is each paragraph about?

Ending
How does the story end?

Have you forgotten anything?

Shorter Writing Test (Non-fiction)
Planning Sheet

Christmas celebrations in the United Kingdom

Write a report for a website about the ways in which people in the United Kingdom celebrate Christmas.

You have 20 minutes. Spend about 5 to 10 minutes planning what you will write. Use the planning guidelines below.

On a flow-chart like this write everything you know about the ways in which people celebrate Christmas in the United Kingdom. Use arrows to begin to organise the pieces of information. This will help you to think of suitable sub-headings.

UK CHRISTMAS CELEBRATIONS

Decide in which person you should write ("we…" or "they…"), how formal or informal your writing should be, and whether it should be mainly active or passive ("we do this" or "this is done").

Make notes of useful words or phrases.

Make notes of useful connective words.

Plan the contents of each paragraph.

Think of a suitable introduction and conclusion.

Spelling Test

This test contains words which are generally known at the end of Key Stage 2; they include many of the spelling strategies, conventions and rules suggested for Year 6 in the National Literacy Strategy *Framework for Teaching*.

> **This test is a short passage with words missed out.**
>
> **You read aloud from page 51 (the answers) – copy the text for ease of use. The missing answers are printed in bold.**
>
> **Your child should write on the test copy on page 48.**
>
> **Allow 10 minutes for the Spelling Test.**
>
> **At the end of the test, give a mark for each correct word and enter it in the space provided.**
>
> **National Curriculum Levels are given on page 51.**

1. Ask your child to listen to you reading the complete text.

2. Ask your child to look at his or her copy of the text. Point out that some of the words have been left out.

3. Tell your child that you are going to read the text again and that he or she should write in the missing words as you read.

4. Read the text aloud again, pausing after each missing word, to give your child time to write it on the test copy. You can repeat each of the missing (bold) words up to three times, if necessary.

47

Spelling Test

Where did Christmas cards _____ ?

This _____ way of _____ seasonal _____ began in the nineteenth _____.

An artist named W C T Dodgson is _____ to have made and sent the first Christmas card, in 1844. It led to the _____ of the first _____ Christmas card by Sir Henry Cole and J C Horsley in 1846. The card showed members of a _____ enjoying a glass of wine (a wassail cup): this was _____ by the Temperance Society, which was doing a great deal of work in cities like Manchester, Leeds and London to _____ people not to drink _____. By the 1870s, _____ cards were _____. They included _____ Christmas _____, symbols such as holly, _____, mistletoe, _____ and _____, as well as the Nativity: the stable, angels and _____.

TOTAL 20

Answers
Reading Test

Question number	Answer	Mark
NON-FICTION		
1	Mexico, Sweden, Nicaragua and Jamaica.	2 for all four, 1 if two or three are named
2	The processions in Nicaragua and Mexico. In Nicaragua, people sing hymns to the Virgin Mary. In Mexico, the processions enact Mary and Joseph's search for somewhere to stay.	2 2
3	Sweden.	1
4	The Yule log and St Lucia's Day in Sweden and the *Jolasveinar* in Iceland.	3
5	Gnomes or elves bring gifts *or* they end on 6 January.	1
6	They made Christmas products for other countries.	1
7	Iceland and Japan. In Iceland, the elves leave presents only for children who have been good; if they have been naughty the elves leave a potato or some other reminder to behave themselves. In Japan, Santa watches what they are doing all through the year.	1 2
8	Nicaragua.	1
9	Yule festivals are about light and warmth. Saint Lucia was a Christian martyr who had a wreath of candles to light her way along dark passages.	3 for a complete answer, 1 if light is mentioned
10	In Iceland, the *Jolasveinar* leave on 6 January, and in Sweden the Yule log is burned until 6 January.	2
FICTION		
1	There was too much choice.	1
2	The person they lived with.	1
3	The food.	1
4	They didn't know who Christ was.	1
5	She didn't know how or where to begin telling them the story of Christ.	1
6	I expect.	1
7	No. They cannot read *or* they have never heard the story of the Nativity.	1 1
8	By golly! By jabbers! Golly! I's sold!	1 for each. Max 3
9	He is stressing that *he knows* how Betty can read the story from the page *or* It is the same as saying "I'll eat my hat …"	1
10	Is I?, I thinks, folks is, Wur it, you was, I's got it, it's the specks that does it, I's sold!, this are. Gooses. You was. Ain't you never heerd?	2 for four, 1 for one to three 1 1 1
11	I specks (I expect), specks (glasses/spectacles), dunna (do not/don't), "polish off" (eat), 'ee (you), ain't (are not/have not), dunno (don't know), nowt (nothing)	2 for four, 1 for one to three
12	Busy and full of Christmas foods. "Crowds of people" and lists of the things the children see, with words which give the impression of large amounts, like thousands, heaps, tons and loads.	1 1
13	Stalls of sweetmeats, tons of toffee, bent upon buying.	2 for all three, 1 for one or two
14	Benny was impressed by the way Betty could read a story from the marks on the pages, but Nelly was fascinated by the story itself.	2
15	He does not use normal spelling, but spells the words in the way in which people said them: ud 'ave (would have), o' (of), dunna (don't), dunno (don't know), an' (and), yer (you), wur (were), heerd (heard), nuthin (nothing), mebbe (maybe), bizness (business).	1 1 for four examples
16	He is a Christian. He calls the story of Christ "the wonderful story". The story suggests that the children ought to know about it.	1 2 for both observations, 1 for one of them
POETRY		
1	Six	1
2	Pudding, mince pies, tree, lights	$\frac{1}{2}$ for each. Max. 2

49

Reading Test Answers

Question number	Answer	Mark
3	Makes pudding; bakes mince pies; shops for presents (packages); decorates a tree.	$\frac{1}{2}$ for each. Max. 2
4	Will the lights work again? We'll have to see!	1
5	Mum. The phrase "such a flurry".	1 for each
6	How we'll endure it I don't know! / Will the lights work again? We'll have to see! / We've never seen Mum in quite such a flurry! Exclamation mark	1 for each line. Max. 3 1
7	The last verse. It is about the Christian belief that Christmas celebrates the birth of Jesus. The others are about festivities.	1 2

Answers
Writing Test

The following criteria provide guidelines to help you gain an idea of your child's Writing Level. A more precise numerical marking system is used by professional markers for marking National Tests.

Each level assumes that the criteria for the previous level have been met.

Content (composition and effect)	Level
Is the writing in the correct form (for example, in an appropriate layout and in the correct person and tense)? Is fiction writing imaginative? Is non-fiction writing clear and does it have a logical structure?	Level 3
Is there an attempt to interest the reader? Is the style or viewpoint maintained throughout most of the writing? Are the criteria suggested on the planning sheet met?	Level 4
Is the tone of the writing maintained throughout? Is the language expressive and effective? Are the vocabulary and language appropriate for the purpose of the writing (for example, the use of technical or subject-based language, metaphors, similes or comparisons)? Are they suitable for the readers?	Level 5
Grammar and structure (sentence structure, punctuation and text organisation)	
Are the ideas presented in sequence, with full stops, capital letters, question marks and commas usually used correctly? Is a greater range of connective words and phrases used (for example, *next*, *afterwards*, *so*)?	Level 3
Are some of the sentences long, with correctly-used connective words and phrases (for example, *meanwhile*, *however*, *which*, *that*, *who*)? Are conditionals, such as *if* or *because*, used? Do some sentences contain more than one verb or include commas, semi-colons, exclamation marks or speech marks? Are the tense and person consistent throughout? Does the structure of the text add to its effect?	Level 4
Are commas and speech marks used correctly throughout? Is a range of connective words and phrases used? Is a range of punctuation marks used correctly, including brackets or dashes and colons to separate parts of a sentence? Is the length of the sentences varied to express meaning? Are passive or active verbs used appropriately?	Level 5

Answers
Spelling Test

Where did Christmas cards **originate**? This **popular** way of **exchanging** seasonal **greetings** began in the nineteenth **century**. An artist named W C T Dodgson is **thought** to have made and sent the first Christmas card, in 1844. It led to the **production** of the first **commercial** Christmas card by Sir Henry Cole and J C Horsley in 1846. The card showed members of a **family** enjoying a glass of wine (a wassail cup): this was **condemned** by the Temperance Society, which was doing a great deal of work in cities like Manchester, Leeds and London to **persuade** people not to drink **alcohol**. By the 1870s, **manufactured** cards were **commonplace**. They included **traditional** Christmas **scenes**, symbols such as holly, **ivy**, mistletoe, **lanterns** and **candles**, as well as the Nativity: the stable, angels and **shepherds**.

National Curriculum Levels
English

Use the conversion tables below to gain an idea of your child's National Curriculum Level in English.

Non-fiction Reading	
Mark	Level
0–7	Below 3
8–12	3
13–18	4
19–21	5

Fiction Reading	
Mark	Level
0–12	Below 3
13–21	3
22–26	4
27–30	5

Poetry Reading	
Mark	Level
0–6	Below 3
7–10	3
11–13	4
14–15	5

Spelling	
Mark	Level
0–3	Below 3
4–6	3
7–14	4
15–20	5

Total marks
Write your child's marks here:

Non-fiction Reading	
Fiction Reading	
Poetry Reading	
Spelling	
Total (maximum 86)	

Approximate National Curriculum Levels for Reading and Spelling

Mark	0–31	32–60	61–74	75–86
Level	Below 3	3	4	5

If your child needs more practice in any English topics, use the WHSmith Key Stage 2 English Revision Guide.

Science Test

Science at Key Stage 2

Most children at Key Stage 2 attain Levels 3 to 4 in Science, but some may attain Level 5. This performance at the different levels is summarised below.

Level 3	Level 4	Level 5
Children can describe differences and provide simple explanations. They can sort materials and living things and offer ideas about why materials are suitable for their purpose. When explaining how things work they link cause and effect, such as suggesting that the lack of light causes plants to become yellow. They also make generalisations about things they see, such as suggesting that it is difficult to see dim lights if they are near very bright lights.	Children can use more scientific terms such as the names of the organs of the body and those of flowering plants. They can use technical terms to describe processes such as evaporation and condensation. They can explain how differences are used to classify materials and living things systematically. They use their ideas about the way the physical world works when explaining how shadows are formed or the way that sound is heard through different materials.	Children can explain the factors behind why different organisms are found in different environments. They can describe the properties of metals and how they are distinct from other materials. They can identify why changes occur in materials and can suggest ways in which specific mixtures can be separated. They can use abstract ideas and models to explain physical phenomena such as the orbiting model of the earth to explain day and year length.

Setting the test

Give your child plenty of time to do the test – 45 minutes should be about right.

The test can be a chance to confirm how well your child has done and how much he or she has learnt. Don't focus exclusively on what the child does not know.

There is a total of 48 marks for the test. Enter the mark in the circle next to each question. Add the marks together at the end of the test. Look at page 62 for an indication of the National Curriculum Level at which your child is working.

Science Test

1 Katie lets a toy car roll down a ramp.
She measures how far it rolls.
She makes the ramp steeper using blocks.
She put her results in a bar chart.

Ramps

a How far did the car travel when the ramp had 2 blocks?

_____

1

b Katie put four blocks under the ramp.
The car went 40 cm.
Draw this result on the bar chart.

1

c Katie tested the car on two different surfaces: a carpeted floor and a wooden floor. She found it rolled further on the wooden floor.

Explain why you think the car rolls further on this surface.

_____

_____

_____

1

TOTAL

3

53

Science Test

Forces

2 Kerrie is checking her bike.
She checks to make sure that the brakes are rubbing on the wheels to make them stop quickly.

a What is the force which slows the bike down?
_____

b One wheel is stiff so she oils the axle.
How does this help?
_____

c Kerrie is not pedalling down the hill.
She is moving fast.
Draw the force of air resistance acting on this bike.

The water cycle

3 Add the correct word to each sentence to explain the water cycle.

evaporates   vapour   rain   condenses   flow

Water falls as _____ and runs into rivers.

Rivers _____ to the sea.

Water _____ into the air.

Water _____ is an invisible gas in the air.

Vapour _____ to form a cloud.

TOTAL 7

54

Science Test

Toughness tests

4 a Children wear out their trousers quickly. Terry wants to test denim and cotton cloth for toughness.

Tick the best way of doing this test.

Rub each one with a smooth piece of plastic. ☐

Rub each one with soap. ☐

Rub each one with a rough stone. ☐

1

b Write down one way to make the rub test fair for each cloth.

_____

_____

_____

1

c Tom tested the hardness of three rocks.

	Can it be stratched with a coin?	Can it be stratched with a steel screw?
Sandstone	no	yes
Limestone	yes	yes
Granite	no	no

Write the names of the rock from softest to hardest.

☐   ☐   ☐

softest ⟶ hardest

1

d Pencil rubbers make holes in some paper when you rub hard. How would you test two types of paper to find the tougher paper?

Write your idea here.

_____

_____

1

TOTAL

4

55

Science Test

Materials

5 **a** Sunil is making toffee. He has a wooden spoon or a metal spoon to stir the hot mixture. Which one should he use?

_____

    b Explain your answer.

_____

_____

    c Masie needs to take some cakes out of the oven. She has rubber gloves or fabric gloves to wear.

Which should she use?

_____

    d Explain your answer.

_____

_____

6 Hamish and Lara are making sandcastles. Hamish has a full bucket of wet sand. Lara has a full bucket of dry sand. Both buckets are the same size.
Explain why Hamish's bucket feels heavier than Lara's.

_____

_____

Food chains

7 Link the correct boxed label to each part of the food chain below. Use each word only once.

| prey | producer | predator | consumer |

lettuce → snail → thrush → cat

TOTAL 9

56

Science Test

8 Tim measured the temperature of the water in his fish tank. He used a sensor attached to a computer to record the changes.

Fish tank

This is Tim's temperature chart.

a How long was the sensor in the tank?

_____

b What was the temperature of the water in the tank at first?

_____

c What was the temperature of the water at 9 p.m.?

_____

d Tim added some warm water to the tank. At what time did he do this?

_____

e Fish tanks are made from glass or plastic. Give **two** reasons why these materials are used.

_____

_____

1

1

1

1

2

TOTAL

6

57

Science Test

Animals

9 a Write a question that will sort these animals into two groups.

ladybird　　　　　bee　　　　　spider

_____

_____

b Gary has listed the stages in the life cycle of a frog. They are in the wrong order.

Number the sentences to show which order they should be in.
(The first has been done.)

The tadpoles change into frogs. ☐

The frogs grow larger. ☐

The eggs grow. ☐

The tadpoles hatch. ☐

The frogs mate and produce eggs. 1

Science Test

Temperature

10 a Amy and Dan are looking at the way in which ice cubes melt.

Amy thinks that the amount of light falling on the cubes is important. Dan thinks the temperature of the air around the cubes is important.

Write how you could test Amy's idea.

_____
_____
_____

2

Write how you could test Dan's idea.

_____
_____
_____

2

b Which things would you keep the same in the tests for Amy's idea?

_____
_____

2

Which things would you keep the same in the tests for Dan's idea?

_____
_____

2

TOTAL

8

Science Test Answers

Question number	Answer		Mark

10a	**You might test Amy's idea by:**
	where possible keeping the two cubes at the same temperature:
	   either
	      putting one ice cube in a dark place and the other in a light place
	   or
	      putting them both in the same light place and covering one with a box.
	You might test Dan's idea by:
	   either
	      putting one cube in a dark warm place and the other cube in a dark cool place
	   or
	      putting one cube in a light warm place and the other cube in a light cool place.
			2
			
			2

10b	**You would keep these things the same for Amy's idea:**
	Two of these:
	  keep both cubes in places which were the same temperature;
	  have the cubes start as the same size;
	  keep them in similar containers.
		You would keep these things the same for Dan's idea:
		Two of these:
		  keep both cubes in places which are lit the same;
		  have the cubes start as the same size;
		  keep them in similar containers.
			2 and 2

10c	30 °C took 15 mins 40 °C took 8 mins		1 1
10d	putting one on a sunny windowsill 4 putting one in the freezer 1 putting one in a fridge 2 putting one in a cool cupboard 3 putting one in hot water 5		4

National Curriculum Levels
Science

Total marks 48

Mark	0–19	20–27	28–38	39–48
Level	Below 3	3	4	5

If your child needs more practice in any Science topics, use the WHSmith Key Stage 2 Science Revision Guide.

Notes

Notes